ISBN-13: 978-1511566865
ISBN-10: 1511566868

ABOUT THE AUTHOR

Rhonda Perryman is a native of Springfield, Massachusetts and currently resides in Atlanta, Georgia. Rhonda is a Real Estate Mogul, Life Coach, Entrepreneur, and Financier. Rhonda has been buying and selling real estate since 1996, residential and commercial real estate has been her specialty for many years. She has worked with several investors and built Million Dollar portfolios. She has managed hundreds of properties. Rhonda has also built, owned and created dozens of successful businesses such as restaurants, retail stores, spa and beauty and construction. Rhonda is also a certified professional life coach and mentor to many.

Rhonda is currently in the preliminary stages of authoring a book and mini-series about her life story as a mom and mogul. Rhonda knows that it's important for people to know your life journey because behind every successful person there are good and bad stories that need to be told. She hopes to inspire others especially the youth and young adults that all it takes is a business license and the will to get started and you can turn your dreams into a reality.

DEDICATION

I would like to dedicate "The Business Kids" Activity Book and Business Plan to all the Self-made Corporations, LLC's, Sole Proprietors and Mom and Pop Businesses. Let's raise our children to be entrepreneurs. The sense of leadership and ownership is a strong foundation for success. Together we can encourage our children to be fireproof. Eliminating the fear of termination has worked wonders in self-development, self-esteem and self-confidence.

Let's encourage our children to be entrepreneurs and eliminate the risk of termination.

Let's make our children Fire Proof!

PUZZLES

Let's Get the Thirsty Kids to the Lemonade.

Start

Finish

Help Business Kids find the Bank.

Finish

Start

Find the Words of Good Business.

Find the Hidden Words.

I	H	C	K	N	Q	P	K	W	A	W	B	T	G
G	C	O	L	O	O	M	I	V	L	V	I	O	O
T	N	R	T	I	T	I	U	S	L	S	N	N	P
B	W	F	X	T	K	O	T	G	M	S	V	L	A
S	B	A	I	A	V	U	Z	A	Y	E	E	G	S
I	T	P	Y	N	M	H	I	S	V	N	S	Y	S
N	R	F	D	I	T	N	T	Z	N	I	T	E	I
H	N	Y	Y	M	D	U	Q	C	P	S	T	N	O
S	I	Q	L	R	R	Q	G	C	A	U	E	O	N
A	I	V	P	E	S	X	L	B	I	B	G	M	M
C	T	Q	P	T	Q	A	N	N	E	O	H	Q	F
E	F	S	K	E	L	L	V	I	V	Y	E	O	C
T	G	B	Z	D	M	S	S	E	C	C	U	S	N
I	O	T	S	S	A	E	D	I	K	N	A	B	Y

BANK	IDEAS	PASSION
BUSINESS	INVEST	SAVE
CASH	MONEY	SUCCESS
DETERMINATION	MOTIVATION	SUIT

How Many Words Can You Make Out of

1. _____
_____
_____
_____
5. _____
_____
_____
_____
_____
10. _____
_____
_____
_____
_____
15. _____
_____
_____
_____
_____
20. _____

Count the words to see what you are.

1-5   You're a Business Owner

6-10   You're an Entrepreneur

11-15 You're a CEO

16-20 You're a "Boss"

Secret Business Code

19 26 9 23

4 12 9 16

26 13 23

14 12 7 18 5 26 7 18 12 13

11 26 2 8   12 21 21

Crossword Unscramble

Unscramble the letters to break the code.
The letters in the box will reveal the answer.

1. DILBU   — — — — —

2. TNOCIUPACO — — — — — — — — — —

3. CESUSCS   — — — — — — —

4. VENETIMTSN — — — — — — — — — —

5. NEMYO   — — — — —

6. ADSIE   — — — — —

7. SANIPOS   — — — — — — —

8. CISNELE   — — — — — — —

Draw a Line to...

What goes together?

 # Draw some items that you would sell in the summer.

Draw some items that you would sell in the winter.

I'm a Realtor

Create Your Own Logo.

(a symbol or other design adopted by an organization to identify its products, uniform, vehicles, etc)

List 10 things a Realtor might need to operate a real estate business.

1. _____

2. _____

3. _____

4. _____

5. _____

6. _____

7. _____

8. _____

9. _____

10. _____

Make Your Own Business Card.

Please include a phone number, address, and business name

Example 1

```
1. _____

2. _____        5.

3. _____

4. _____
                                    6. _____

                                    7. _____
```

1. Company Name

2. Address

3. Phone Number

4. Email Address

5. Logo

6. Website

7. Slogan

Create your own slogan.

A short and striking or memorable phrase used in advertising

" You start packing and we'll make it happen. "

1 _____

_____

_____

2 _____

_____

_____

3 _____

_____

_____

Create Your Store Sign.

I'm a Restaurant Owner

Cookies and Cupcakes

Create Your Own Logo.

(a symbol or other design adopted by an organization to identify its products, uniform, vehicles, etc)

List 10 things a Restaurant Owner might need to operate a restaurant.

1. _____

2. _____

3. _____

4. _____

5. _____

6. _____

7. _____

8. _____

9. _____

10. _____

Make Your Own Business Card.

Please include a phone number, address, and business name

Example 1

```
        1. _____

2. _____          5.

3. _____

4. _____
                                    _____ 6.

                                    _____ 7.
```

1. Company Name

2. Address

3. Phone Number

4. Email Address

5. Logo

6. Website

7. Slogan

Create your own slogan.

A short and striking or memorable phrase used in advertising

" You start packing and we'll make it happen."

1

2

3

Create Your Store Sign.

I'm a Store Owner

Create Your Own Logo.

(a symbol or other design adopted by an organization to identify its products, uniform, vehicles, etc)

List 10 things a Store Owner might need to operate a store.

1. _____

2. _____

3. _____

4. _____

5. _____

6. _____

7. _____

8. _____

9. _____

10. _____

Make Your Own Business Card.

Please include a phone number, address, and business name

Example 1

1. _____

2. _____

3. _____

4. _____

5.

6. _____

7. _____

1. Company Name

2. Address

3. Phone Number

4. Email Address

5. Logo

6. Website

7. Slogan

Create your own slogan.

A short and striking or memorable phrase used in advertising

" You start packing and we'll make it happen. "

1 _____

_____

_____

2 _____

_____

_____

3 _____

_____

_____

Create Your Store Sign.

My Business Plan.

Name of Business _____

Address of Business _____

Phone Number _____

Nature of Business _____

Description of Daily Operations _____

Projection of Startup Cost _____

Brief Forecast of Return of your Investment (Profit)

_____

_____

_____

_____

Send your business plan to

thebusinesskidsbp@gmail.com

Do you want to be a business kid?

Log on to the business kids fan page on Facebook.

Log on to:
www.magictouchlifecoaching.com

Look for contest details for a chance to win the opportunity to start your first business.

VISIT
WWW.MCBRIDESTORIES.COM
FOR MORE TITLES

Made in the USA
Middletown, DE
07 December 2015